INTRO

I0111487

Written by Dean Koon who has played guitar and bass guitar for 50 years, worked with many name groups, backed up artists and songwriters, done countless recording sessions in Memphis, Muscle Shoals, Tupelo, and Nashville; worked on the road, worked on "Mornin'" (a TV show in Tupelo, Mississippi), got his degree in music education, taught public school and lessons over 30 years in addition to writing many songs he recorded; as well as independent artists. Dean taught 14 years at two community colleges teaching beginner guitar using the knowledge he gained from the many years playing music. He saw the many books that were on the market and wanted to write his own easy to learn "roadmap" to guitar. He says if you'll learn the basic chords, the chords in the different keys, and the most used progressions, you'll be able to play 1000's of songs!

IT MAKES LEARNING AND PLAYING MUSIC FUN!

It may take a month to learn this info or three years. Just start, practice and keep going even if your fingers get sore, as they'll get better after a few weeks. Get with some other friends to play, buy "Play Along" CD's; **Have Fun** and **Keep Playing**!

When you buy your guitar make sure buy a guitar tuner, have your salesperson tune your guitar and show you how to tune it.

ACKNOWLEDGEMENTS

I've had the good fortune to have played music with some of the best musicians and groups around, done countless recording sessions, worked on the road and done tv work. Along the way I put my music degree and my "playing" degree together to come up with an easy and simple method to learn guitar. I used this method to teach classes and individuals in a country music program at a community college then later in night classes. This method collapses time frames so the student learns the basics quicker.

My mentor was Johnny Wiginton who is one of the most well-known guitarists in the South. We played music together every day in the studio and doing gigs usually 6 nights per week! All the playing helped me learn the keys, chords and progressions. This is the "roadmap" to playing guitar and successful learning. If a student knows the scales, the keys and the chords in those keys he/she can play 1000s of songs. You already know pretty much where the song will go from that!

I would also like to acknowledge Bill Rutledge who taught piano and music theory at NE Community College, Tammy Smith for doing the setup for this book and Brad Bullock for the final touches, illustrations and expertise.

Finally, I'd like to thank all the students I taught over the many years. Without the students this book would not be possible.

- Correct way to hold your pick: Make a fist with your right hand (or if you're left handed use your left hand). Next, pop your first finger out some so that the first finger and thumb make an "O". Hold the pick where they meet. Don't plant any fingers on the guitar body, as it will slow you down.

This is your guitar fretboard showing your six strings biggest to smallest and the frets.

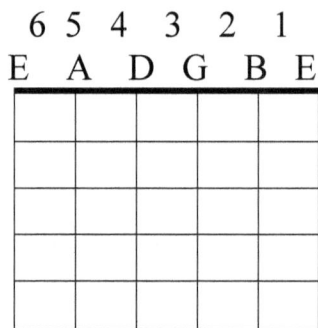

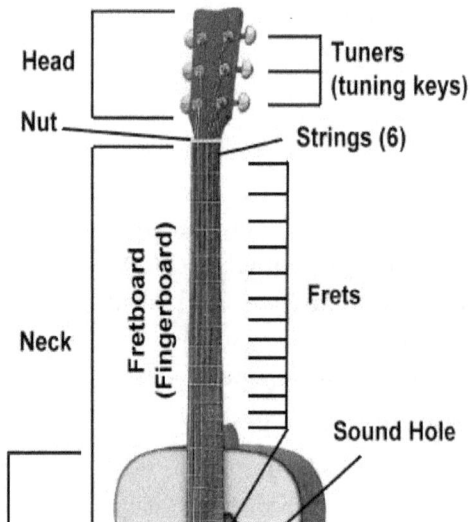

Top to Bottom

The strings are:

	E	A	D	G	B	E
	Biggest 6th	5	4	3	2	1 (smallest)

On your left hand you have thumb, 1st, 2nd, 3rd and 4th fingers.

- For a simple **G chord**, place your 3rd finger left hand ring finger on the third fret 1st string.
  Mash down firmly in the middle of the fret. Strum the first four strings.

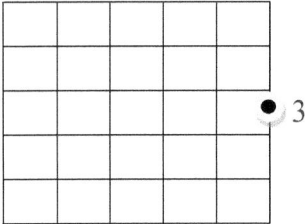

- For a **G7 chord** place your 1st finger on the first string first fret. Strum the first four strings.

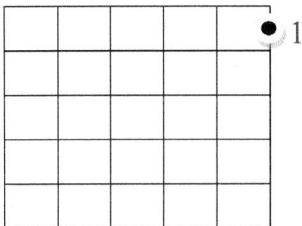

Practice strumming G four times, then G7 four times. Pat your foot with each strum. Your hand and foot should do the same thing.

- For a **C chord** place 1st finger on the 1st fret second string.

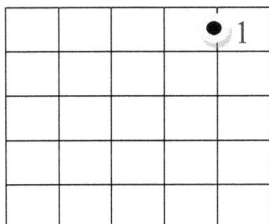

Play 3 strings

- *Play G four times, G7 four times, C 4 times, then repeat. Go Slow!

- For a **D7 chord** place 1st finger on 1st fret 2nd string, 2nd finger on 2nd fret 3rd string and 3rd finger on 2nd fret 1st string.

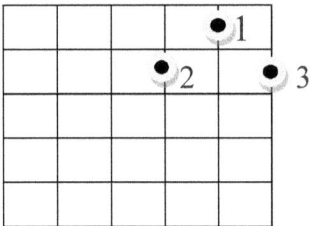

Play 4 strings

- Practice making C, playing it four times. Leave the 1st finger on, add your 2nd and 3rd fingers for D7. Play it four times.

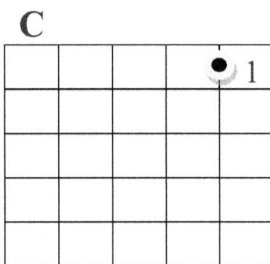

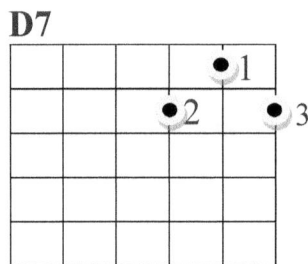

C   D7

- Practice strumming G four times, G7 four times, C four times, then D7 four times.

  Practice these four chords strumming each four times. Pat your foot like you're slowly walking. Get it so you don't miss a beat changing from one chord to the next.

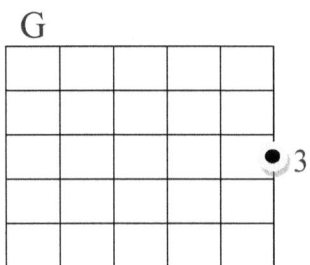

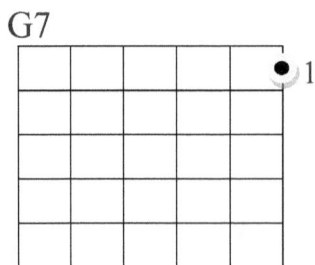

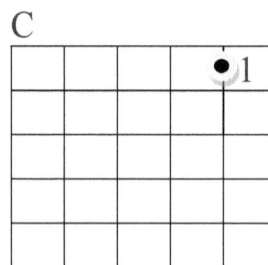

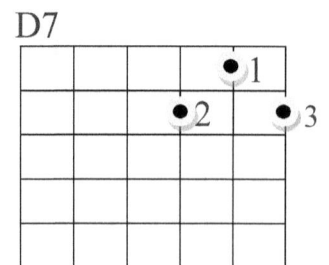

G   G7   C   D7

- For an **A minor** chord:
  1st finger on 1st fret second string
  2nd finger on 2nd fret 4th string
  3rd finger on 2nd fret 3rd string

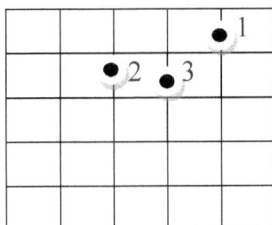

Strum 5 strings

- For an **E chord**, which is the same for an A minor, just up a string each finger:
  1st finger on 1st fret 3rd string
  2nd finger on 2nd fret 5th string
  3rd finger on 2nd fret 4th string

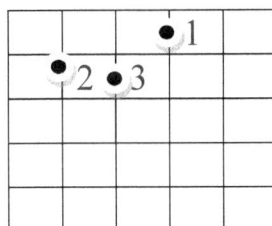

Play all 6 strings

- *Practice playing A minor four times then <u>moving each finger up a string</u> to make E. Play E four times.

Am

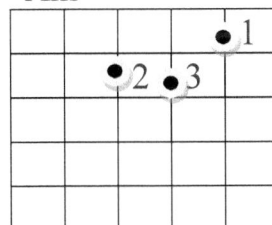

E

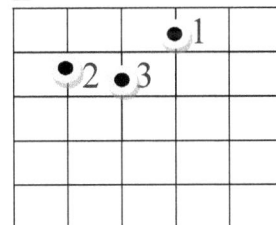

- For **E minor**:
  2nd finger - 2nd fret - 5th string
  3rd finger - 2nd fret - 4th string

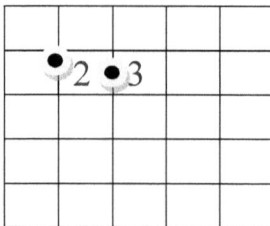

  Play all 6 strings

- For an **A chord**:
  1st finger - 2nd fret - 3rd string
  2nd finger - 2nd fret - 4th string
  3rd finger - 2nd fret - 2nd string

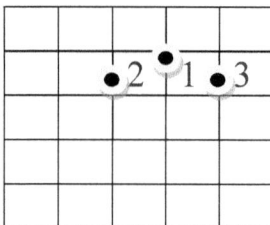

- **D Chord**:
  1st finger - 2nd fret - 3rd string
  2nd finger - 2nd fret - 1st string
  3rd finger - 3rd fret - 2nd string

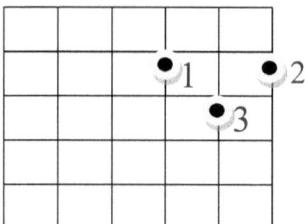

- **B7**
  2nd finger – 2nd fret – 5th string
  1st finger – 1st fret – 4th string
  3rd finger – 2nd fret – 3rd string
  4th finger – 2nd fret – 1st string

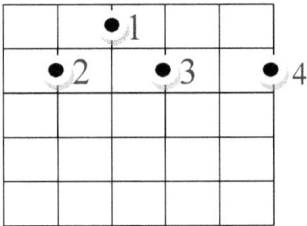

  •1
  •2 •3 •4

  Play 5 strings

- **B Minor**
  1st finger – 2nd fret – 1st string
  2nd finger – 3rd fret – 2nd string
  3rd finger – 4th fret – 3rd string

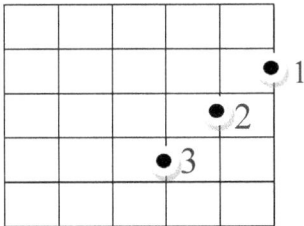

  •1
  •2
  •3

- **F chord** – This one may take awhile:
  Hold 1st and 2nd strings – 1st fret with 1st finger
  2nd finger – 2nd fret – 3rd string
  3rd finger – 3rd fret – 4th string

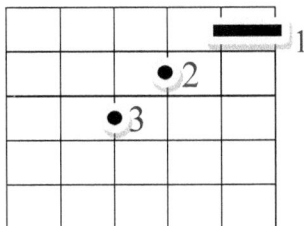

  1
  •2
  •3

  Play 4 times

You may have to get the first two strings to sound and keep practicing until the other two strings sound. This took me awhile. It's a key chord.

- Full **G chord**: You can use either 1, 2, and 3 fingers OR 2, 3, and 4. I use 2nd, 3rd and 4th.

Full **G chord**: You can use either 1st, 2nd, and 3rd fingers OR 2nd, 3rd, and 4th. I use 2nd, 3rd and 4th.

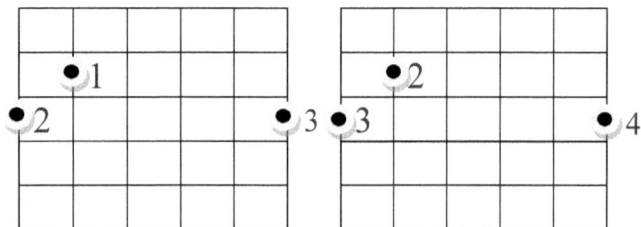

- **G7 chord**:
  1st finger – 1st fret – 1st string
  2nd finger – 2nd fret – 5th string
  3rd finger – 3rd fret – 6th string

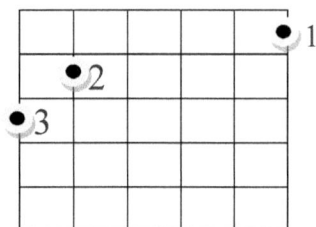

- **C Chord**

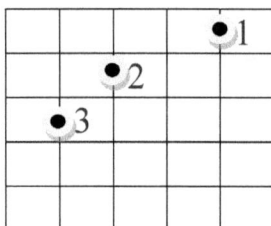

  1st finger – 1st fret – 2nd string
  2nd finger – 2nd fret – 4th string
  3rd finger – 3rd fret – 5th string

Those are your basic chords! For photos of finger placements see last page.

Practice strumming each four times, then changing. Next, practice strumming each chord one time then changing. The faster you can change the better!

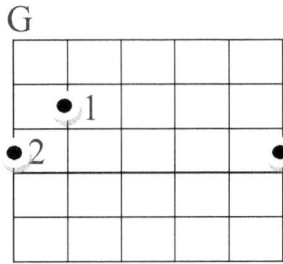

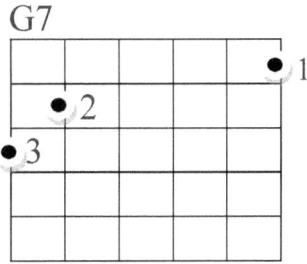

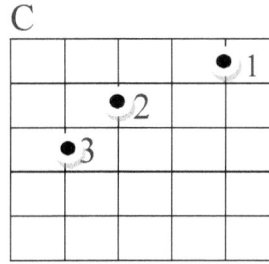

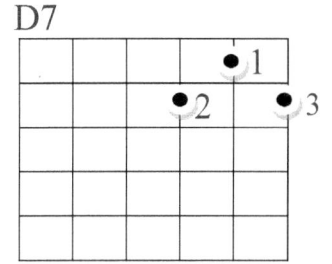

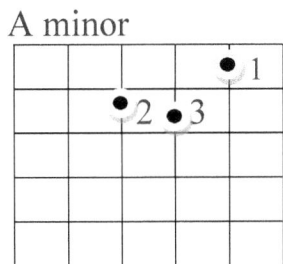

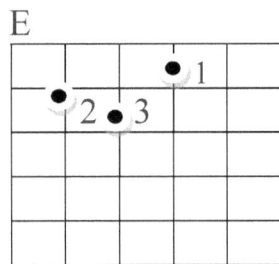

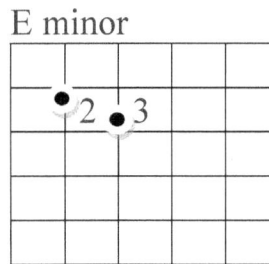

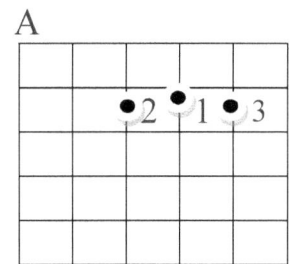

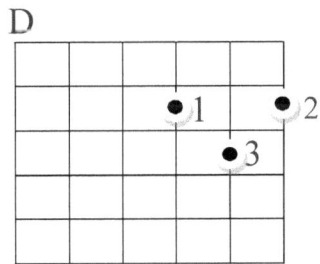

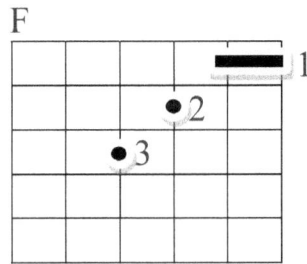

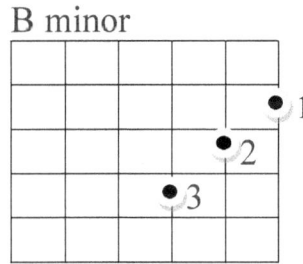

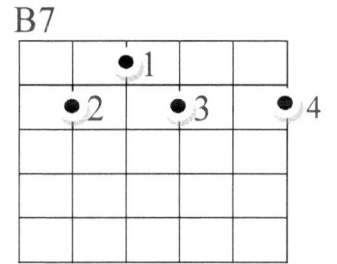

G   G7   C   D7

A minor   E   E minor   A

D   F   B minor   B7

Learn these and you'll be ready to learn 1000's of songs!!!

- Now for progressions – a group of chords that progress from one to another like in songs.

1. G   C

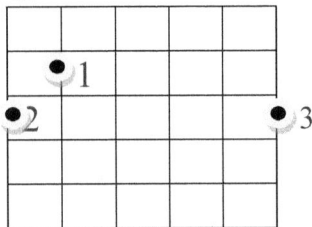   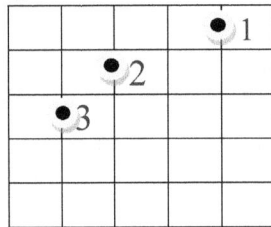

Repeat

2. G   D7

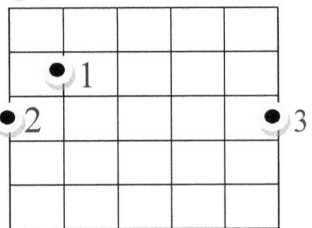   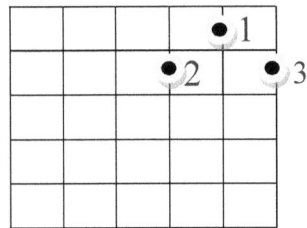

3. G   C   D7   G

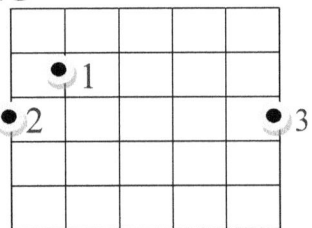   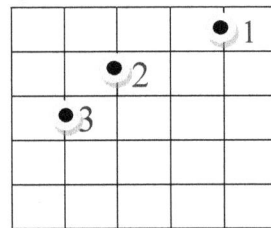   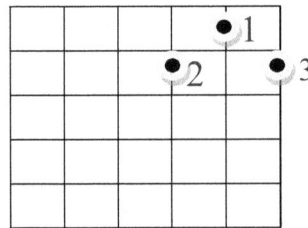   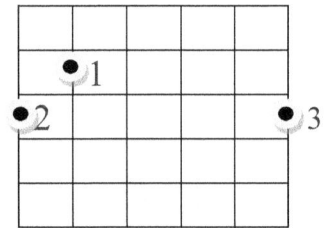

4. G   A minor   D7   G

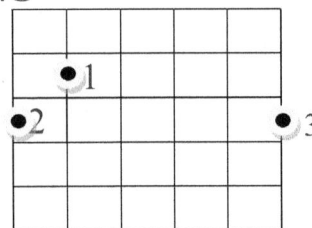   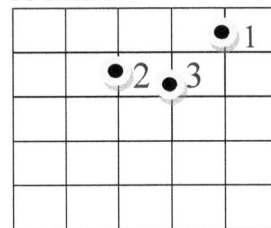   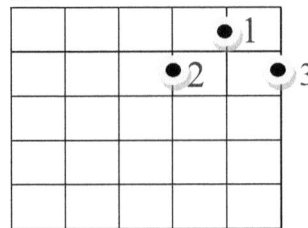   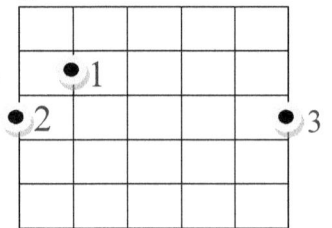

5. G 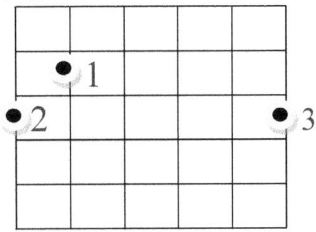   E minor 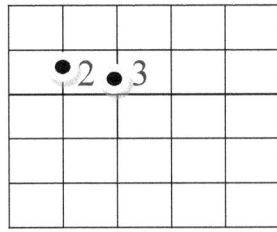   C 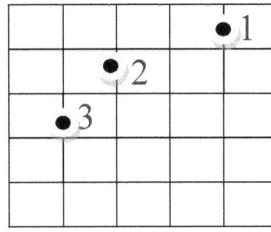   D7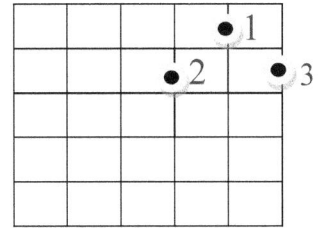

G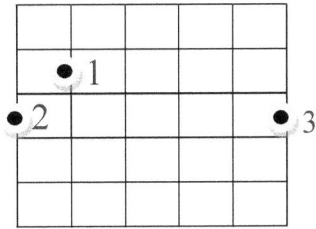

6. D 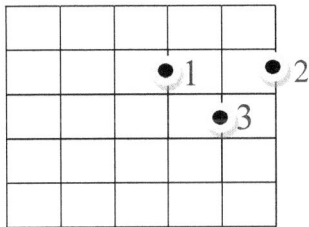   G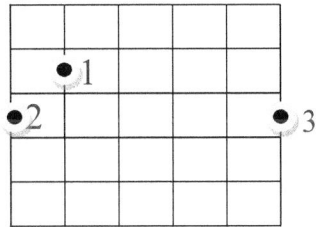

7. D 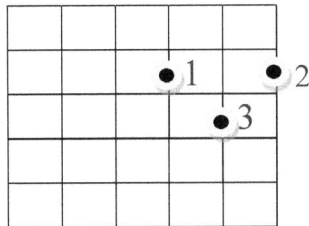   A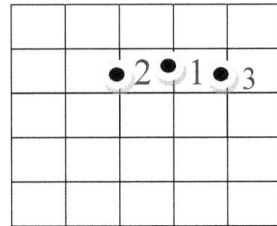

8. D 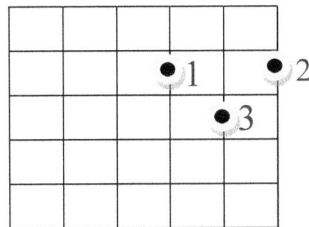   G 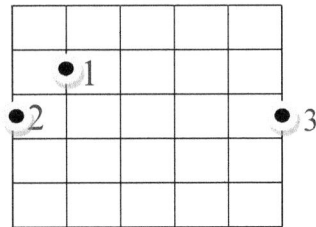   A 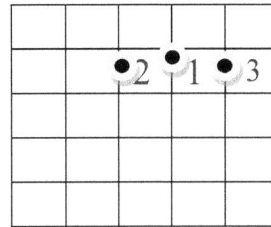   D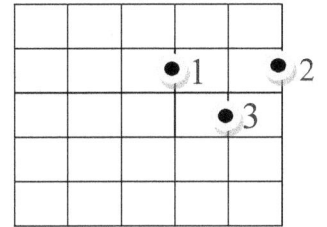

9. D   E minor   A   D

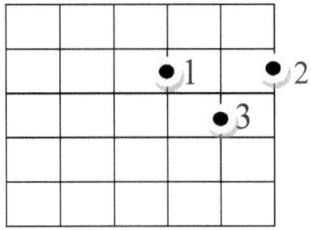 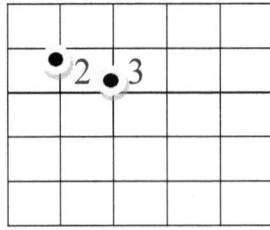 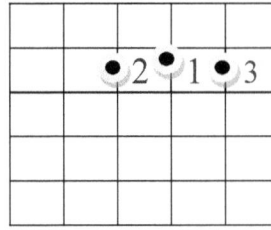 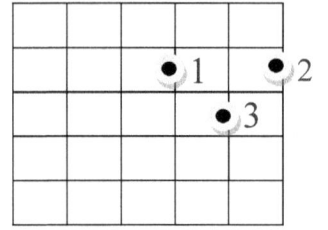

10. D   B minor   G   A

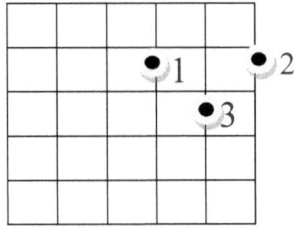 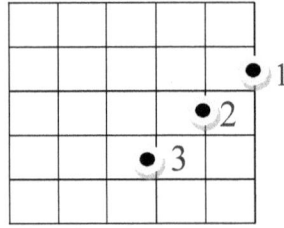 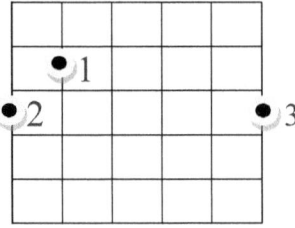 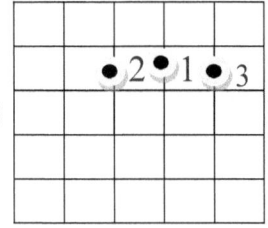

D

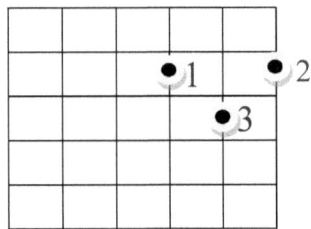

11. A   E

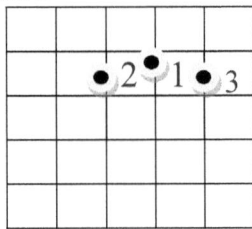 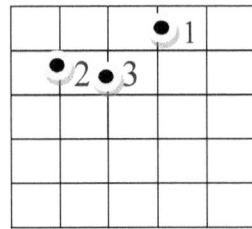

Repeat

12. A   D

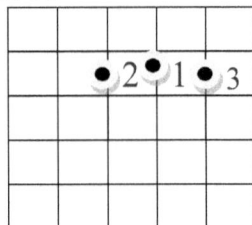 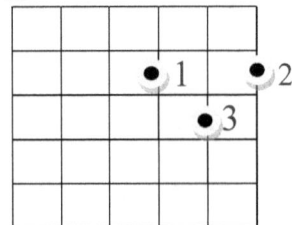

12

13. A   D 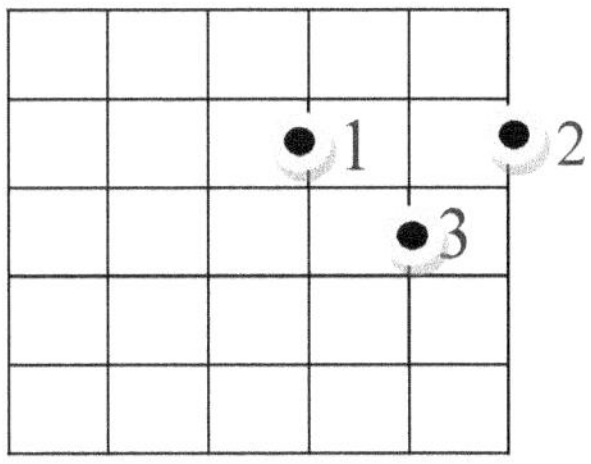   E 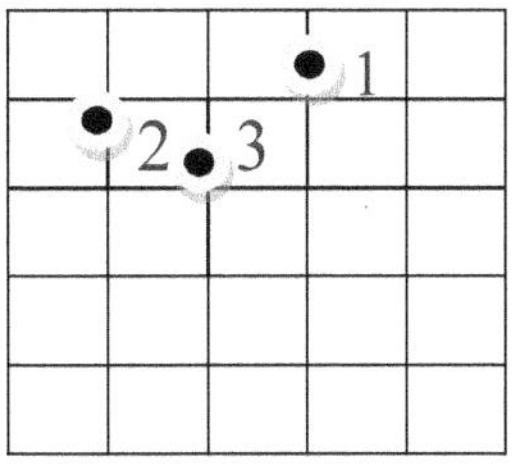   A

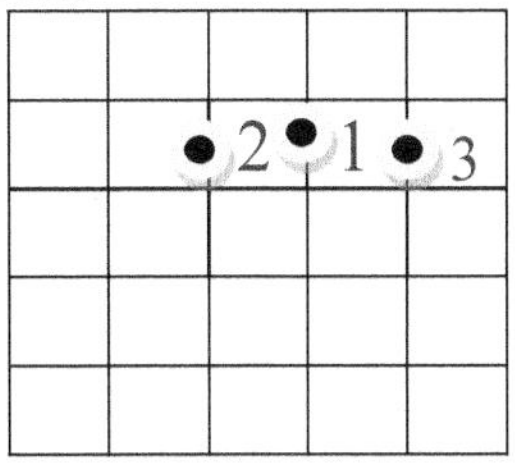

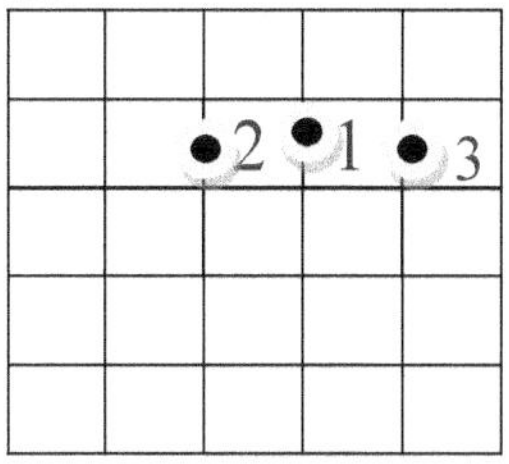

14. A 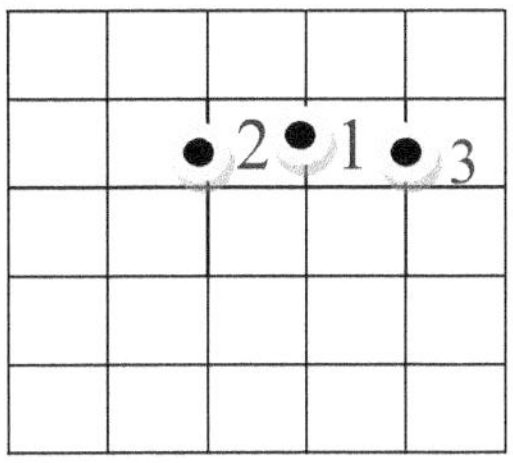   B minor 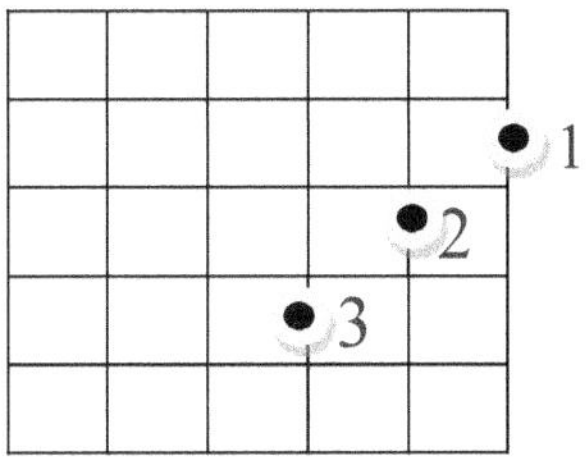   E 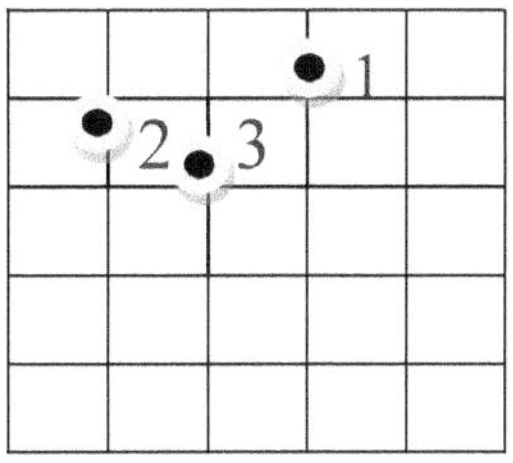   A

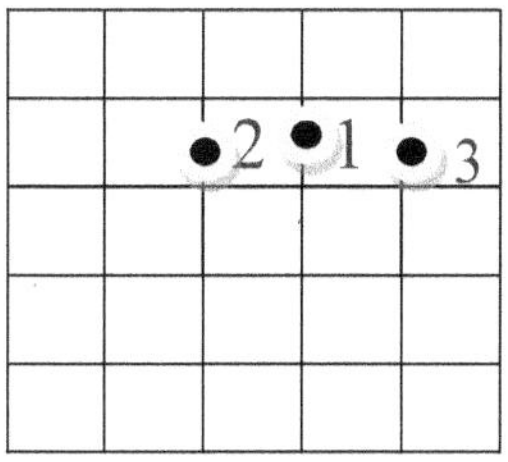

15. A 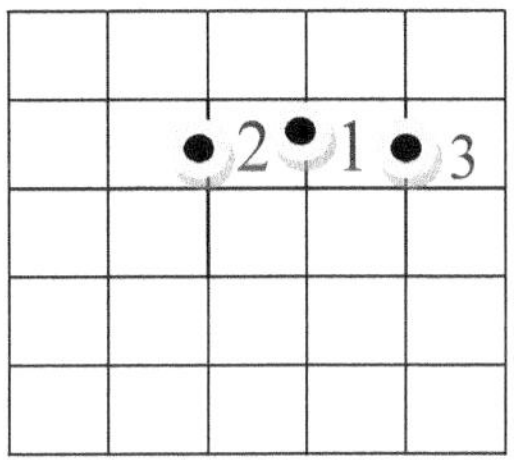   F#minor 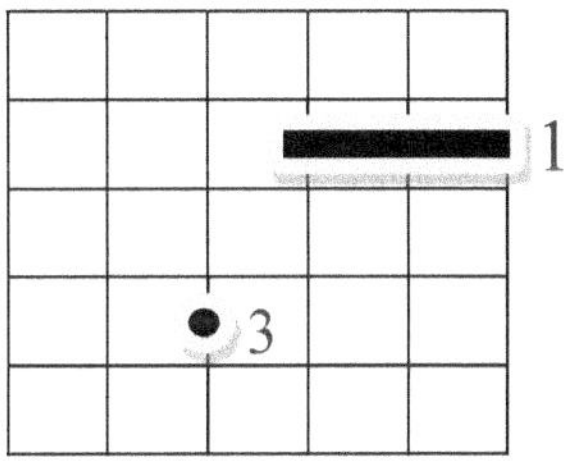   D

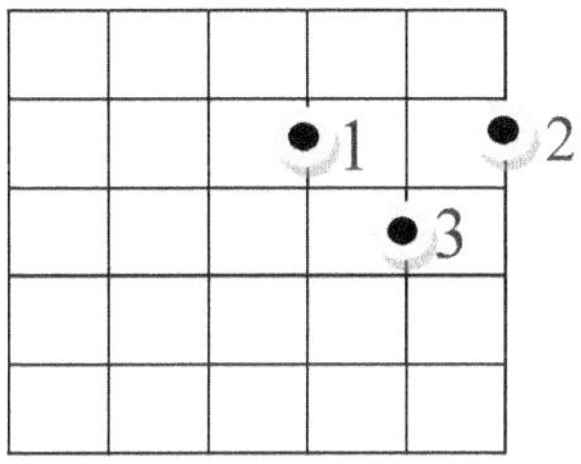

E 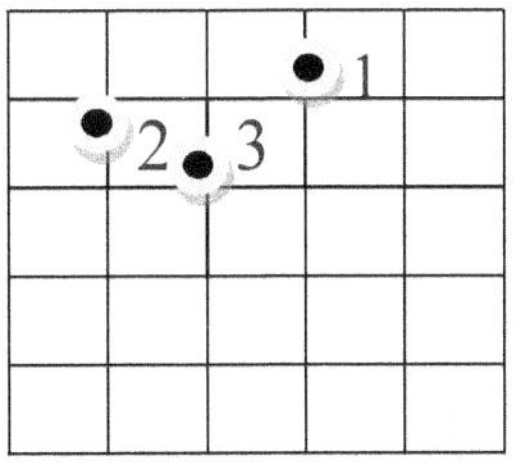   A

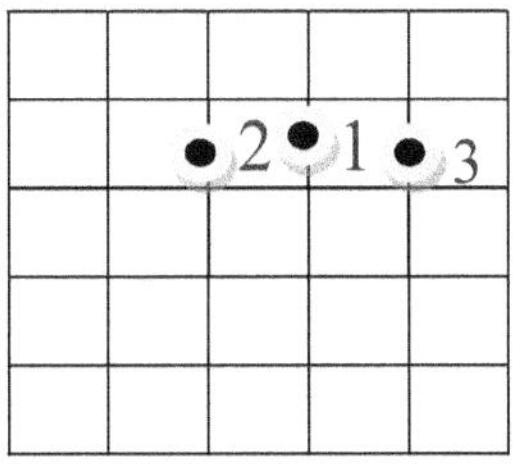

16. E 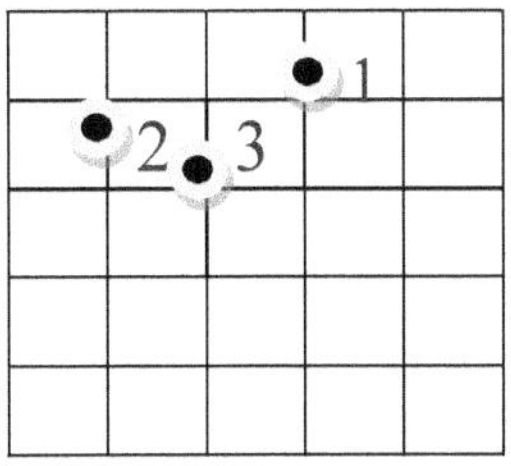   B7 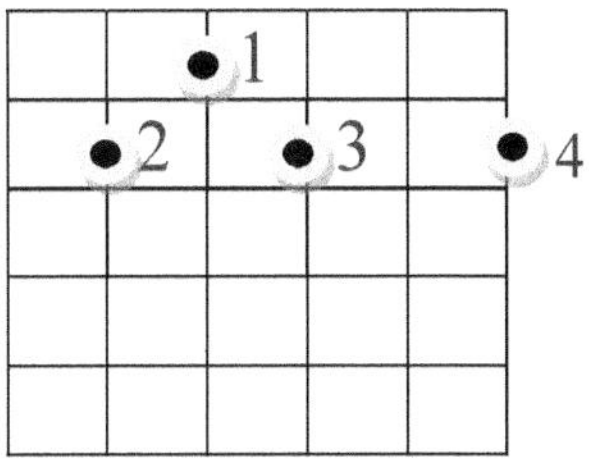   E

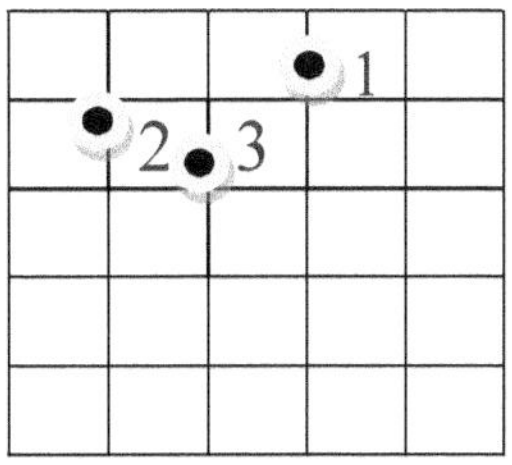

17. E   A   B7   E

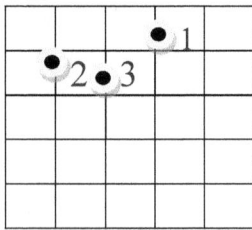 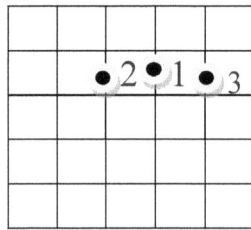 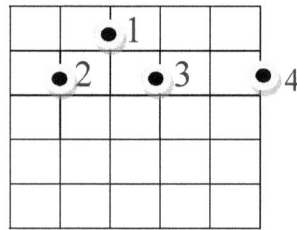 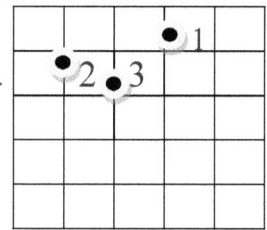

18. C   F

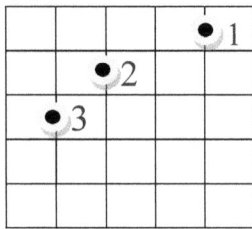 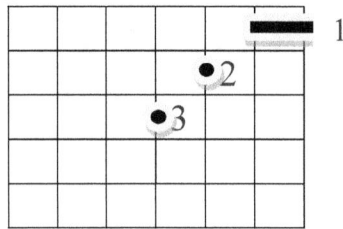

19. C   G7

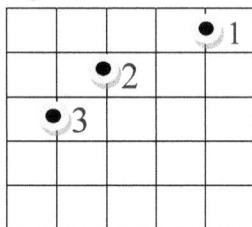 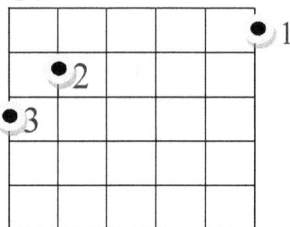

20. C   F   G7   C

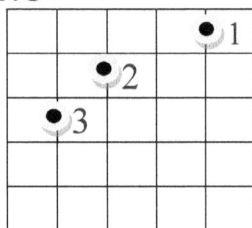 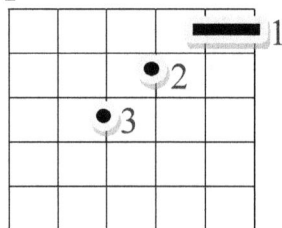 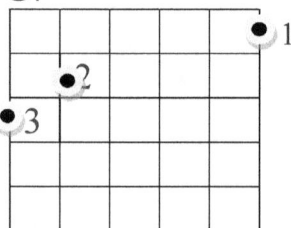 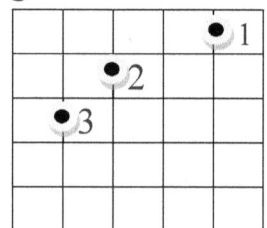

21.C   A minor   F   G7

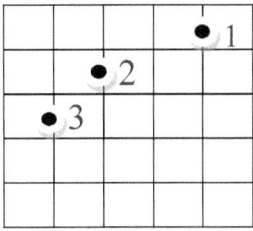   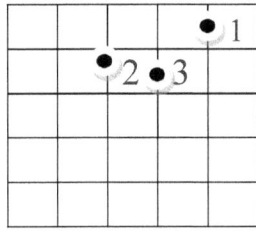   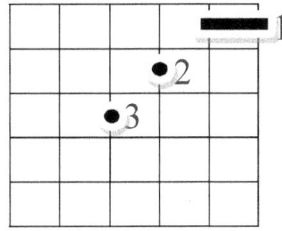   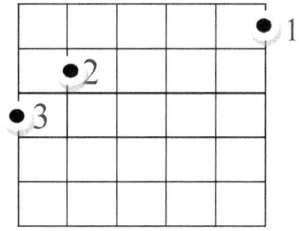

C

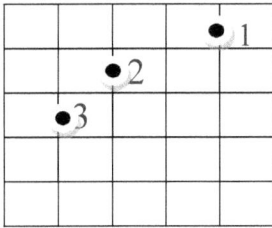

22.F   C7   F

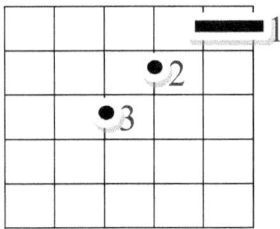   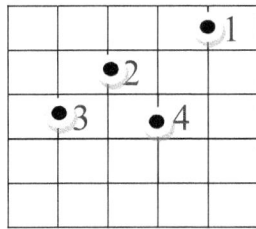   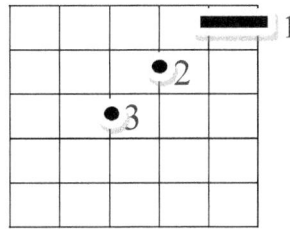

23.F   Bb   C7   F

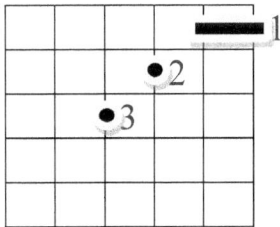   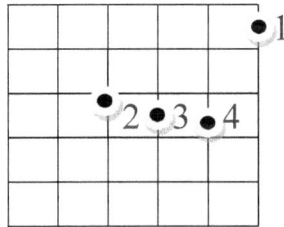   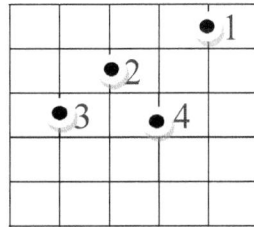   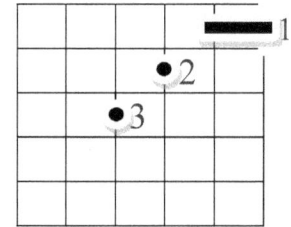

Practice playing these four times each, then one time each until you're comfortable.

15

- Remember when you are playing one chord to the next to pat your foot slowly just like you're walking. Strum with each pat so that your wrist is going down towards to the floor as your foot goes down. When you can change from one chord to the next without missing a beat, **you're getting good**!

- To advance with your strumming when you can do the changing without missing a beat you need to start doing up and down strumming. When you pat your foot it goes down and up. So does your hand. Practice down and up some without strumming your guitar. Next make a full "G" chord. Practice down up down up down up until it's smooth.

- Now go back and practice your progressions using down up. This is the most used strumming.

CHROMATIC SCALE. This is really important and if you will learn this it will help you as you get better. A chromatic scale on guitar for example is like playing the first string open then playing each fret all the way up to the 12th fret. That's E to E or an octave. So from E first string open which is E, you have E, F, F#, G, G#, A, A#, B, C, C#, D, D# and E.

The way you can learn how to do a chromatic scale is to remember your alphabet. It starts with A and goes A, B, C, D, E, F, G, A. If you go up from A, let's say on the 5th string, it will be A, A#, B, C, C#, D, D#, E, F, F#, G, G#, A. NOTICE THE B AND E AREN"T USUALLY SHARPED. It's just the way it is for now. If I ask you to build a chromatic scale starting on D like on the fourth string…it would be D, D#, E, F, F#, G, G#, A, A#, B, C, C#, D. Got it? The reason the chromatic scales are so important is this- each chord that you've learned will turn into 12!!!! If you make a D chord and slide each finger up one fret you will have D#. If you move each finger up another fret you will have E…then F, F#, G, G#, A, A#, B, C, C# and D!!!! It's the same fingering but you move that chord up one fret each time. If you make an F chord and move up one fret you'll have F#...move up another fret you'll have G, etc..then G#...A, A#, B, C, C#, D, D#, E, and F.

This comes in handy when you're singing a song and it's too low and you need it to be in a higher key. Most guitar players especially those who play acoustic guitars use a CAPO. Let's say you are in the key of G but it's too low and needs to be a little higher. A way to solve that problem is to place a capo on the first fret behind the first fret and secure it. You play G but now it sounds G#!!! If you were playing G, C, and D for the song without the capo, you place the capo on the first fret and play the same chords here but it's a little higher and still sounds great! If it's still too low you move the capo to the second fret and play G, C, and D, but it will sound A, D, and E!!! Got it? It really comes in handy. You can actually play almost any song in the key of G, D, or C by using a capo!! You just have to learn how to do it.

Here's your "MAP TO SUCCESS"! Memorize these scales, even if you have to write them until you know them. You'll see 5 basic keys and the ones most used.

G	A	B	C	D	E	F#	G
C	D	E	F	G	A	B	C
D	E	F#	G	A	B	C#	D
A	B	C#	D	E	F#	G#	A
E	F#	G#	A	B	C#	D#	E
F	G	A	Bb	C	D	E	F

Now these are the corresponding chords in each of the above keys:

G	Am	Bm	C	D	Em	F# diminished	G
C	Dm	Em	F	G	Am	B diminished	C
D	Em	F#m	G	A	Bm	C# diminished	D
A	B	C#	D	E	F#	G# diminished	A
E	F#m	G#m	A	B	C#m	D# diminished	E
F	Gm	Am	Bb	C	Dm	E diminished	F

* Because the 7th step where the diminished chords appear are not used often those are replaced with these chords. These are the most used in country, rock, gospel, etc. Notice the numbers. Also notice some of the same chords are in different keys so when you learn one chord it's used again and again. Most players don't know this lineup when they start. If you can learn these you will know where most songs will be going so that when someone says this is in G you'll already know the chords. Realize that the minor chords can also be made major chords and sometimes the majors can be minors. This took me a long time to learn and you can know it in hours.

1	2	3	4	5	6	7	1
G	Am	Bm	C	D	Em	F	G
C	Dm	Em	F	G	Am	Bb	C
D	Em	F#m	G	A	Bm	C	D
A	B	C#	D	E	F#	G	A
E	F#m	G#m	A	B	C#m	D	E
F	Gm	Am	Bb	C	Dm	Eb	F

NOTICE THE NUMBERS ABOVE THE CHORDS....This is the NUMBER SYSTEM. Let's say your song is in C and the chords are C,F and G. That's 1, 4 and 5. If it's too low go up to D and play 1,4 and 5 which will be D, G and A. If you have C, Em, F and G which is 1, 3, 4 and 5 in C and it's too low you can take it up to D and play D, F#m, G and A. You can play any combination of chords or numbers in one key they play them in another. This comes in handy when a vocalist says the song is too low or too high you can use the numbers. Later when you're familiar you can just write the numbers down. Makes it very easy. ALSO if you'll learn this system and you're on stage and one of the group says this song is 1, 5, 6, 4 for example you'll know what to play.

1. G   D   Em   C
   G   D   C   C

2. G   G   C   G
   G   G   C/D7 G

3. G   D   Am   C
   G   D   C   C

4. G   G   C   G
   G   G   D7   D7
   G   G   C   G
   Em   D7   G   G

5. D   Am   G   Em

6. G   G   G   G
   C   C   G   G
   G   G   G   Em
   G   D7   G   G

7. Am   C   D   F
   Am   C   E   E
   Am   C   D   F
   Am   E   Am   Am

8. Am   G   F   E

9. Am   Am   Am   Am
   Dm   Dm   Am   Am
   E   Dm   Am   Am

BEAUTIFUL CHORDS

1. C Maj 7   F Maj 7

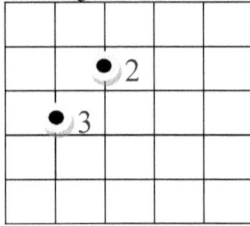 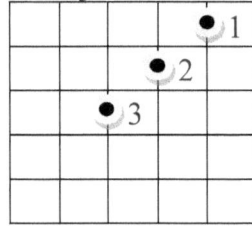

2. D Maj 7   G Maj7

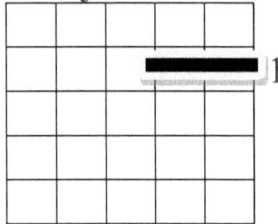 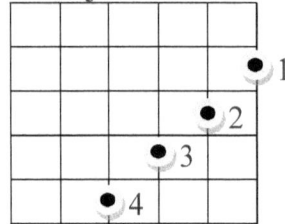

3. A Maj 7   D Maj7

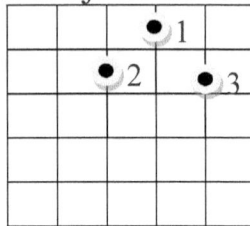 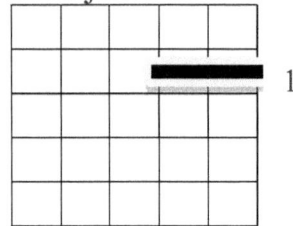

4. G Maj 7   C Maj 7

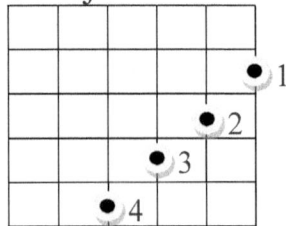 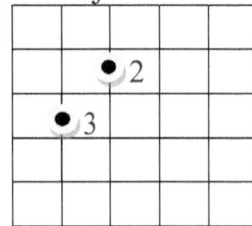

5. G   G Sus 4

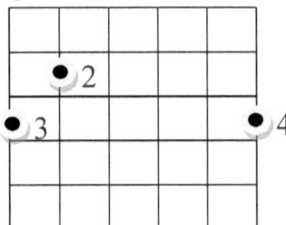 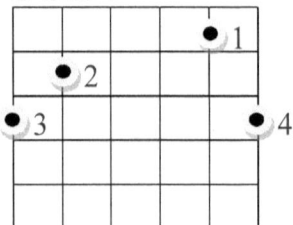

20

6. C   C Sus4

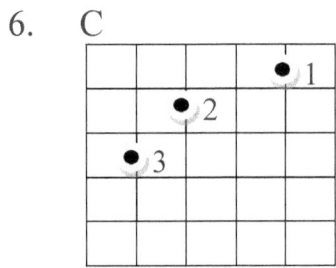 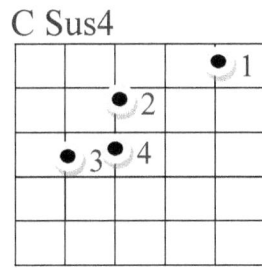

7. D   D Sus4

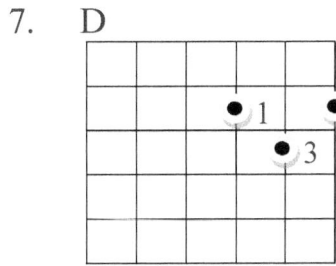 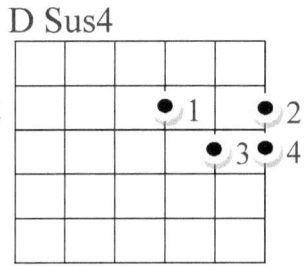

8. A   A Sus4

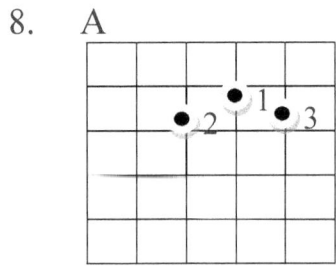 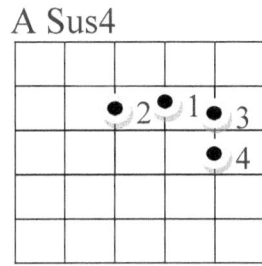

SOME MUSIC THEORY WITH SHARPS, FLATS AND NATURALS

Let's take the single note G. It's the third fret on the first string. Since it's called G we say that's G natural or simply G. If you play the fret behind G or the second fret that's G flat or Gb. If you play the 4th fret or the fret past G you have G sharp or G#. Flats lower the pitch while a sharp raises it. This works with chords also. If you play a D chord and move it back one fret you have D flat=Db. If you move your D chord up one, that will make a D#.

When you have a note or chord that can have two names but one tone or sound, that's called enharmonic. For example, on the first string open you have E then F on the first fret, F# on the second fret and G on the third fret. From above if you move that G note back one fret you have G flat (Gb). Well that's also F#. It has one tone or one sound but it can be called two different notes. If you'll make an F chord and move it up one fret you have F# and it can be called Gb also. The difference will be in which key the song is in.

So you'll know - Ab and G# sound the same, A# and Bb, C# and Db, D# and Eb, F# and Gb also sound the same.

KEY SIGNATURES - if you see a song book or sheet music here's a way to tell what key you're in:

- C has no flats or sharps

- G has 1 sharp

- D has 2 sharps

- A has 3 sharps

- E has 4 sharps

- B has 5 sharps

- F# has 6 sharps

- C# has 7 sharps

- F contains 1 flat

- Bb has 2 flats

- Eb has 3 flats

- Ab has 4 flats

- Db has 5 flats

- Gb has 6 flats

- Cb has 7 flats.

A way to remember the sharps and flats is: C has no flats or sharps; then G, D, A, E, B, F# and C#. The flats go F, Bb, Eb, Ab, Db,Gb, Cb.

NUGGET - you can usually see that if a song has no flats or sharps and the song starts with a C chord you're in the key of C; but each home key has a relative minor just like we have brothers, sisters or cousins. There's only one note difference in the home key and the relative minor. If you look at the key of C you have:

1	2	3	4	5	6	7	1
C	Dmin	Emin	F	G	Amin	Bb	C

The 6th step or A minor is the relative minor. If a song starts in A minor and uses D minor and E major for example then you're playing in A minor or if the song uses A minor, G, F and E major for example. The relative minor is always the 6th step of the key.

NUGGET - if you'll keep playing, all this comes together and it makes playing so much easier and enjoyable because you know what you're doing and you'll get to where when you hear a song you'll know what key it's in and hear the chord changes too! This is your "ROADMAP". Learn it and use and KEEP PLAYING!

Bass Notes and Chords:

You need to know the bass notes that go with the basic chords. There are many ways you can use this option.

- For D (same 2 bass notes work for D minor, D7, D major 7, etc.)

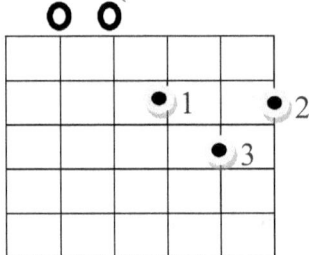

The root or first bass note is the 4th string open which is a D note. The alternate bass note is the 5th string open. Practice playing the 4th string first, then the chord, then the 5th string and the chord so you have bass note/chord then bass note/chord, or bass note on 1 and 3 chord on 2 and 4.

You'll find that whatever bass note you play usually the alternate bass note is right above it. There are a few exceptions.

- For A

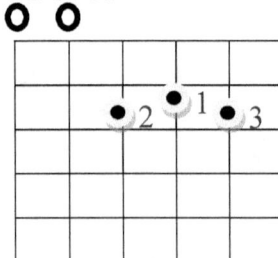

Root is the 5th string open – alternate is the 6th string open.

- For E

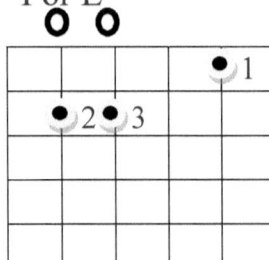

Root is the 4th string – 2nd fret. Alternate is the 5th string 2nd fret. Also, you play the 6th string open for the root then the 5th string 2nd fret for the alternate.

- For C

Root is the 5th string 3rd fret. Alternate is 6th string 3rd fret. You can move your 3rd finger on the 5th string up a string to play the alternate or make your chord like this:

Then play the 5th string and alternate 6th string.

- G

Two ways – you can play the 3rd string for the root then 4th string for the alternate or play the 6th string 3rd fret you already have and the 4th string for the alternate.

- For F

Play the 4th string 3rd fret for the root then move your 3rd finger up a string to play the alternate.

- For B minor

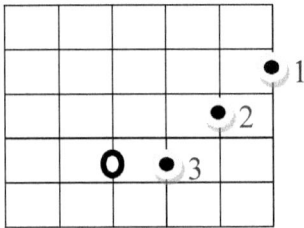

Root is the 3rd string 4th fret. Move your 3rd finger up a string for alternate or add your 4th finger.

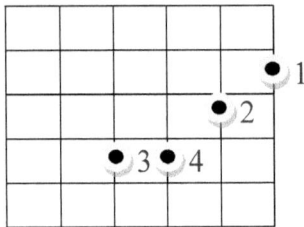

Play the 3rd string for the root. Play the 4th string for the alternate.

Use your pick. Play the bass note then chord then alternate and the chord.

Start using your fingers on the right hand to do the same. Make a D chord. With your thumb, play the 4th string. Next, with your 1st finger on the 3rd string, your 2nd finger on the 2nd string and your 3rd finger on the 1st string. Play those three strings for the chord by bringing the three fingers upward a little. Try to keep all four fingers close to the strings and use small strokes. Next, with your thumb play the 5th string for the alternate, then play the chord with your 1st, 2nd and 3rd fingers. Go slow to make it smooth.

- To start using your fingers more make the D chord.

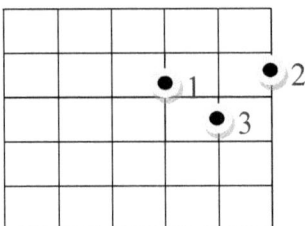

With your thumb on the 4th string: 1st finger on the 3rd string - 2nd finger on the 2nd string - 3rd finger on the 1st string. Lightly play the 4th, 3rd, 2nd, 1st, 2nd, 3rd strings in that order. Do this until it's smooth. Keep your fingers close to the strings. There's so much you can do using your fingers and many songs that use this style.

These are your basic chords as described on pages 1-9

G chord

G7 chord

C chord

D7 chord

A minor chord

E chord

E minor chord

A chord

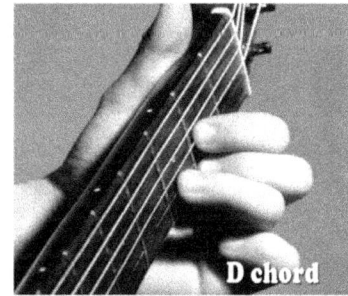
D chord

B7 chord

B minor chord

F chord

Full G chord

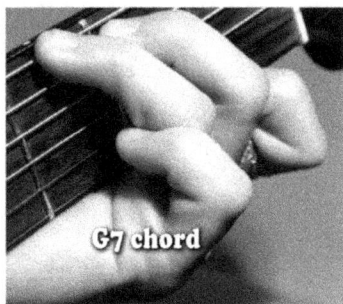
G7 chord

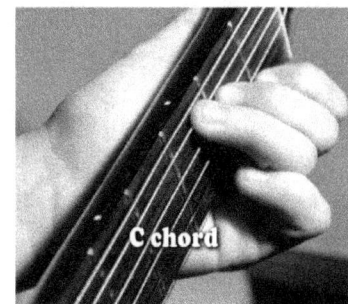
C chord

27